The big book of ideas
By George Gibson
Illustrations by YOU!
ISBN 978-0-244-44031-2

I0461798

Welcome to this book. In this book you will get some ideas to draw and fill it. Thank you for purchasing it and I hope you enjoy it.

Tips: I would suggest not using felt tips or sharpies on the inside pages. Instead use crayons, ball tip pens and pencils. I would suggest using something to seal your drawings.

Fill this page with...

...your favourite things.

Make this page scary.

Smudge this page

Make this page...

...using only things from nature

MAKE THIS PAGE FANCY

Fill this page with words

Try some African art

Use only a ball point pen and make a masterpiece

Do some scrap booking on this page

Use a fat tip pen

Fill this with your dreams

Fill this with people you love

Use some bubble writing

Do some doodles

Do some pop art

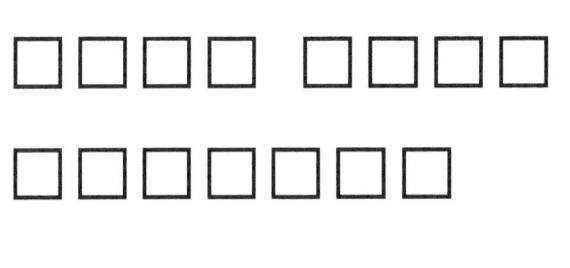

STAIN THIS PAGE

Make this page sticky

Use some shapes

Decorate this page with something Christmas

Draw your pets

Draw your favourite place

Do something spotty

Do some caveman art

Use something recycled

Do something with pom-poms

Use condiments to
paint(ketchup, mustard
ext)

Use your favourite pen to draw

Use some paint

Do something random

The end

Wow well done you finished! I hope you enjoyed decorating this book and I hope it inspired you. Make sure you keep an eye out for any more books I make in the future.

Thanks

www.ingramcontent.com/pod-product-compliance
Lightning Source LLC
Chambersburg PA
CBHW061235180526
45170CB00003B/1310